The

Family Records Centre

Introduction to

Family
History

Public Record Office
Kew
Richmond
Surrey TW9 4DU

© Crown Copyright 1999

ISBN 1 873162 80 4

A catalogue card for this book
is available from the British Library

Produced in association with Halpen Limited
Introduction photography © Hugh Alexander

Contents

Introduction

The Family Records Centre (FRC) was set up as a joint service by the Public Record Office (PRO) and the Office for National Statistics (ONS) in April 1997.

For the first time two of the key sources for the study of family history have been brought together in one building - the indexes to births, marriages, deaths and adoptions (previously in the General Register Office search room at St Catherine's House) and the nineteenth century census returns for England and Wales (previously at the Public Record Office search room at Chancery Lane).

The modern building housing the FRC is set in the heart of historic Clerkenwell, conveniently situated near the London Metropolitan Archives and the Society of Genealogists.

However, the FRC aims to be more than just a centre for researching these sources. Visitors receive advice and information on the wide range of sources for the study of family, local or social history which are located beyond the FRC in other record offices and institutions.

On the first floor at the FRC a series of illustrated information panels assists many first-time users researching their family history. These panels have proved so popular that we have produced this adaptation of them in booklet form.

We hope that this guide will inspire those about to start their own family history research, serve as an aid to more experienced researchers and give a flavour of the many interesting sources of information available.

Margaret Brennand
and Marily Troyano
PRO and ONS Centre Managers
Family Records Centre

Where to find us

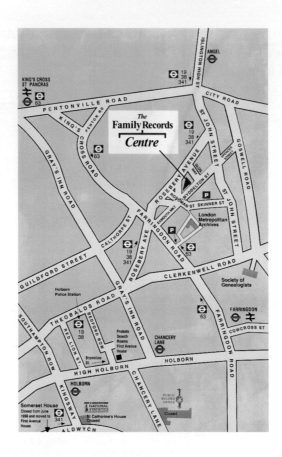

Family Records Centre
1 Myddelton Street
London EC1R 1UW

Census and General enquiries
Telephone: (0181) 392 5300
Minicom: (0181) 392 5308
Fax: (0181) 392 5307
PRO Web site: http://www.pro.gov.uk/

Births, Marriages, Deaths enquiries
Telephone: (0151) 471 4800
Minicom: (0151) 471 4530
ONS Web site: http://www.ons.gov.uk/

Starting your search

All family historians, be they professional genealogists or people exploring their own family tree, have to start their search somewhere. The Family Records Centre has been established as a centre for family history research.

Before coming to the FRC, the keen family historian should have started his or her personal search at home, following up small domestic clues that are to be found in the most ordinary surroundings.

Gravestone inscriptions like this one at Chaldon in Surrey can provide information

Very often a person or event, from however long ago, is powerfully evoked by studying old photographs, a personal possession, letters, or an inscribed family Bible. Members of the family may be recalled to life through a set of medals at home, a family joke or story repeated endlessly at Christmas get-togethers, or a haunting epitaph on a tombstone.

At the Family Records Centre, you can see many of the documents that will allow you to piece together your family history. Here are names, dates, descriptions in black and white. The family legend suddenly takes on a new light of reality.

The following pages tell you about the many different types of records which you might use in your search, what kind of information you can get from them, and where they are held.

If you are interested in more detailed information on any particular topic, Public Record Office information leaflets deal with subjects in greater depth. We have also made some suggestions as to books which we think are useful, in the 'Further reading' list on pages 25 and 26.

We have made every effort to ensure that titles mentioned are either available for consultation in the library at the FRC, or at the Public Record Office in Kew, or are for sale in our bookshops.

Diary entry of
Captain Mark Sweny, RN, 1916

If you have any doubts or questions, please do not hesitate to approach the FRC or the PRO - we are here to advise and guide you.

An old photo will often reveal valuable clues to the family historian

Surnames

Family history is made possible because we all have surnames.

Surnames on a muster roll of 1441 *(PRO ref. E 101/53/33)*

Spellings have tended to change with the passage of time. Although spellings became more standardised from the nineteenth century onwards, prior to this, surnames could vary greatly according to local pronunciation or a scribe's literacy.

Some family historians concentrate on one surname. If you are interested in studying a particular surname, you can contact the Guild of One-Name Studies.

Surnames are second names, developed in the Middle Ages and used to identify individuals in legal records. By the sixteenth century, with the exception of Wales, their use in the UK was universal.

Most British surnames are derived from one of the following sources:

• Place names, indicating where someone came from, such as Scott or Cornwall.

• Descriptions of where people lived, such as Greenwood, Lane, Croft or Grange.

These two groups of geographical descriptions account for about fifty per cent of British surnames.

• Occupations, such as Tailor, Fowler, Mercer, Sawyer, Archer, Smith (the abundance of Smiths being due to the many different types of occupation given this name, eg blacksmith, swordsmith, silversmith).

• Nicknames, such as Short, Brown or Redhead, which often referred back to peasant or village origins.

• Patronymics, such as Robinson, Pritchard or MacDonald, which were usually derived from the father's first name.

• Foreign names, such as Beecham (Beauchamp) or Stone (Stein).

Medieval archer
(PRO ref.E 36/274)

Right: Elton John's Deed Poll document *(PRO ref. J 18/458 p7)*

Surnames can change

Some people choose to change their surname officially, by Deed Poll, and many documents recording the changes can be found at the Public Record Office at Kew.

The main reason for a change of surname, however, is marriage, when most women take their husband's surname. A woman's maiden name can usually be found on her birth and marriage certificates.

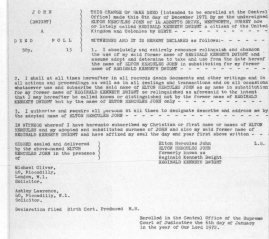

Births, marriages and **deaths** after **1837**

From 1st July 1837, the state took responsibility for the registration of all births, marriages and deaths in England and Wales. However, registration was not compulsory until 1874.

To start tracing your family tree, you should begin with the more recent events which are to be found in these records, and follow them back through the generations.

Birth, marriage and death certificates give you details of when and where these events occurred. Birth certificates will also give you parents' names, mother's maiden name and occupation of the father; marriage certificates will give you the occupation, address and age of the couple, together with the names and occupations of the fathers; and death certificates will give you the cause of death, marital status of women, and age of the deceased. In the case of children, parents' names are also given.

Oscar Wilde's death certificate, Paris 1900 (*PRO ref. RG 35/35*)

A typical birth certificate

Where the records are

The Family Records Centre holds indexes of registers for births, marriages and deaths in England and Wales from 1837, up to about twelve months ago. They are records of separate events and are not indexed together in families.

They are to be found on the ground floor at the FRC, where staff are available to help you with queries and applications for certificates which can be collected or sent to you by post within four working days.

You will also find at the FRC the following *indexes:*

• legal adoptions in England and Wales since 1927

• births, marriages and deaths among members of HM Forces or persons attached to them. Some records extend as far back as 1761

• deaths in the Boer War, 1899–1902

• deaths of English and Welsh servicemen in World Wars I and II

• births and deaths at sea on any UK-registered ship, since 1837

• births and deaths in UK-registered aircraft, since 1949

• births and deaths aboard British-registered hovercrafts or on off-shore installations

• births, marriages and deaths of British subjects in foreign and Commonwealth countries, registered by Consuls or High Commissioners

• Registrar General's miscellaneous returns of births, marriages and deaths of Britons at sea and abroad, 1627–1960

You can also consult, for a fee, the birth, marriage and death indexes for Scotland since 1855 although certificates must be ordered from Edinburgh.

The system also allows access to the indexes of Scottish divorces since 1984 and old Scottish parish birth and marriage indexes.

Census

A census is an accurate head-count of the population of a country on one particular night. The census was established in the UK in 1801, and has been taken every ten years ever since, except in 1941.

The information was originally used to study population growth, its effect on the economy and wealth of the nation, and to assess future educational requirements.

A census enumerator complains about the poor pay, 1851 (*PRO ref. HO 107/1531*)

From 1841, however, they can provide a mine of information for the family historian, including: name, age, occupation, from 1851 place of birth, marital status and relationship to the head of the household.

Census records can be used to trace family mobility and can reveal previously-unknown family relationships.

The census records everyone living or staying in a house on one particular night (*Miss Amy Miles's Dolls House, 1887, © Board of Trustees, Victoria & Albert Museum*).

The early census returns, from 1801 to 1831, did not contain much personal information and were simply population counts; most were later destroyed.

Returns for England, Scotland and Wales are not available for public consultation until they are 100 years old. Census returns for 1901 will therefore be available in January 2002.

Where the records are

Microfilm copies of the complete Census of Population returns for England and Wales, from 1841 to 1891, are available on the first floor at the Family Records Centre. There is a consolidated personal name index for 1881.

Surviving census returns for 1801–1831, of which there are very few, can be found in county record offices.

The indexes to the 1881 and 1891 Censuses of Population in Scotland can also be consulted at the FRC, using the Scottish Link terminals on the ground floor. There is a fee for this service. The actual returns of these and other Scottish censuses are kept in Edinburgh. The few Irish records which have survived are available in Belfast and Dublin.

Microfilms of census records for the local area can be seen at county record offices and local study libraries. They are also available at family history centres run by the Church of Jesus Christ of Latter-day Saints (Mormons).

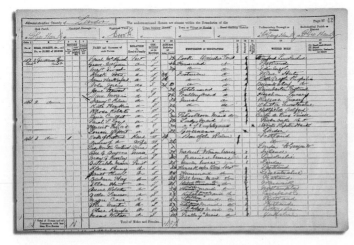

Census return of the Duke of Portland's household, 1891 (*PRO ref. RG 12/69*)

Wills, Letters of administration and Death duty registers

A will is a legal document in which a person specifies how his or her property should be distributed after their death.

Wills are a useful source of personal detail, not only about the status and occupation of the person who made the will, but also about links with family, friends, and executors. They deal with land, its ownership, money, goods and chattels, and animals.

The Prerogative Court of Canterbury was up to 1858 the most senior ecclesiastical court in the country and 'proved' or validated a great number of wills. The other major court was the Prerogative Court of York. Prior to 1858, wills were also proved in a number of smaller diocesan or archdeaconry courts.

Letters of administration (often abbreviated as 'admons') are a document granted when a person has died without making a will ('intestate') or when a will was invalid (eg, if it was not signed, or if one of the witnesses was a beneficiary). Letters of administration give authorisation for administering the personal estate of the deceased.

Letters of administration are issued for purely practical reasons and, unlike wills, do not give us much information. They usually refer solely to the name, marital status and residence of the intestate, the name of the person to whom letters of administration have been granted, and their relation to the deceased, if any.

Death duties are taxes paid to the Inland Revenue on a deceased person's estate. They were first levied in 1796.

Indexes to death duty registers can help you find a will, as they can tell you in which court the will was proved or letters of administration granted.

Death duty registers were kept until 1903. After that date, the registers were replaced by individual files for each deceased person, which were kept for thirty years and then destroyed. This is still the practice.

Frontispiece of a volume of wills produced by the Prerogative Court of Canterbury, 1562 *(PRO ref. PROB 11/46)*

Where the records are

The Family Records Centre holds microfilm copies of the wills and letters of administration proved at the Prerogative Court of Canterbury from 1383–1858. Wills proved at the Prerogative Court of York can be seen at the Borthwick Institute of Historical Research. Many other wills can be found at local record offices.

All wills for England and Wales, from 12th January 1858, are held at the Probate Search Room, First Avenue House, High Holborn, London.

Death duty registers up to 1857 and indexes from 1796–1903 can be seen at the Family Records Centre. The registers from 1858 are available at the Public Record Office, Kew.

Isaac Newton's Letters of Administration, 1728 *(PRO ref. PROB 6/103)*

Parish registers

Parishes are ecclesiastical districts based around a church. Parish registers - which keep a record of the baptism, marriage and funeral ceremonies taking place at that church - are still kept to this day.

In 1538, during the reign of Henry VIII, the clergy were instructed by Thomas Cromwell to keep parish records of baptisms, marriages and burials, which were to be written up weekly. The records were stored in the parish chest, for which two keys were kept, one by the parish priest and one by the churchwarden. From 1598 onwards, copies of all entries in the registers had to be sent to the Bishop's Registry every year - these copies are called Bishops' Transcripts.

The information contained in parish registers can vary in quality and legibility, depending on the person who was compiling it. In addition, registers are rarely complete and many are missing, although substitutes can sometimes be found in Bishops' Transcripts.

During the latter half of the seventeenth century and particularly during the eighteenth century, there was a decline in the Church of England congregation, and many people chose to worship at other churches or chapels, collectively known as 'non-conformist'. There is further information on non-conformist or 'non-parochial' registers on page 14.

Burial register of victims of the Great Plague, 1665, parish of St. Mary, Whitechapel *(by permission of the Rector of Stepney and Corporation of London: London Metropolitan Archives, ref. P93/MRY1/59)*

The parish church of St Peter & St Paul, Chaldon, Surrey

Where the records are

Parish registers are now found mainly in county record offices. Between 9,000 and 10,000 transcripts of parish registers are also held by the Society of Genealogists.

Indexes to Scottish births and marriages from 1553–1854, however, are available at the Family Records Centre, on the computerised link to the General Register Office, Scotland, and on CD-Rom as part of *Family Search*.

The International Genealogical Index, which can also be consulted at the Family Records Centre, contains information about baptisms and marriages taken from many parish registers.

Bishops' Transcripts which have survived can be found in county and diocesan record offices.

A useful finding aid is *The Phillimore Atlas & Index of Parish Registers*, which is available in the FRC and PRO libraries.

Baptisms

Baptism is a ceremony whereby a person is admitted into the church and named.

The earliest baptismal registers, dating from Tudor times, also often serve as a record of birth. High infant mortality made speedy baptism advisable, as well as a legal requirement.

Up to the nineteenth century, when civil registration began, parish registers of baptism usually give the child's name, father's name, sometimes the place of abode, and the date of baptism, which generally took place within two weeks of birth.

From 1812, they invariably provide the mother's name, and the father's abode and occupation.

Baptism register 1788, parish of St. Marylebone (*courtesy of the Rector and Churchwardens of St. Marylebone and Corporation of London: London Metropolitan Archives, ref. P89/MRY1/9*)

Marriages

In 1753 Lord Hardwicke's Marriage Act compelled all citizens to marry, by banns or by licence, in the Church of England (with the exception of Quakers and Jews). It is from this date, therefore, that marriage registers become an important source of information for the family historian.

For the first time, marriages were recorded in a separate register and 'banns books' were kept. These recorded the public announcements that had to be issued before a marriage could take place, in case anyone knew of any legal impediment to the marriage, such as bigamy or a close blood relationship between the bride and groom. Register entries now also showed marital status and parishes of residence, and had to be signed by the couple and by witnesses.

Marriage registers before 1754 usually record the couple's names and, occasionally, marital status or the fact that one of the parties lived in another parish.

The most useful index to baptism and marriage registers is the I.G.I. (International Genealogical Index), which can be consulted at the FRC.

Marriage register 1836, parish of St. Luke, Chelsea, including marriage of Charles Dickens (*courtesy of the Rector and Churchwardens of St. Luke's, Chelsea and Corporation of London: London Metropolitan Archives, ref. P74/LUK/208p.67*)

There are various collections of marriage indexes, which could be of help to you. Many are available at the Society of Genealogists.

Burials

Early burial register entries usually give only the name of the deceased, except in the case of children, where the father's name was normally entered. Burials of still-born children were often not recorded.

In the eighteenth century, some non-conformist cemeteries came into being, so after this date not all burials appear in parish registers.

Burials do not normally appear in the International Genealogical Index.

Burials register 1841, parish of St. James, Pentonville (*courtesy of A.E.Harvey, Barnsbury Team Ministry and Corporation of London: London Metropolitan Archives, ref. P76/JS2/31p.89*)

Non-conformist registers

'Non-conformist' is a term describing religious denominations outside the established Church of England and includes Methodists, Congregationalists, Baptists, Presbyterians, Unitarians and Quakers. The term is sometimes also applied to Roman Catholics and Jews.

Quaker marriage certificate, 1690 (*PRO ref. RG 6/1277*)

Florence Nightingale's birth certificate, Dr Williams's Library, 1820 (*PRO ref. RG 5/83*)

Protestant dissenters' burial register, 1795 (*PRO ref. RG 8/305*)

The records of birth, baptism, marriage and death or burial of people from these denominations are referred to as 'non-conformist' or 'non-parochial' registers, and are a rich source of genealogical information for many families. It is important to bear in mind, however, that non-conformists did sometimes use the Church of England for legal reasons, especially for marriages between 1754 and 1837

Between 1742 and 1837, many non-conformists registered the birth of their children with Dr Williams's Library in London.

Following Lord Hardwicke's Marriage Act of 1753, many non-conformists chose to marry by 'licence', which meant that they were legally married but were not obliged to attend Church of England services to hear their banns being called.

The annotation in an Anglican parish register 'marr. by lic.' is therefore a possible indication that the parties were non-conformist, particularly if no baptisms follow of any children.

Some congregations also had their own burial grounds. A number of registers have survived.

In 1840, the Non-Parochial Register Act required non-conformist registers to be handed over to the state, and most were gradually collected in despite the reluctance of some denominations.

Where the records are

Many non-conformist registers can be seen at the Family Records Centre. Much of the information they contain, with the exception of that on Quakers, has also been captured on the International Genealogical Index, available for consultation at the FRC.

County and diocesan record offices often hold registers dating from 1837 or before, but many are in an incomplete condition and others have simply been lost.

Schools and apprentices

Schools

In 1870, provision was made for the education of children up to the age of ten in England and Wales, although attendance did not become compulsory until some ten years later.

Once you have found out which school your ancestor attended, you will find school registers an excellent source of information, with their insights into the intimate details of everyday life: the age when children entered and left school, academic progress, reasons for absences or leaving, what jobs they went into, medical notes, descriptions of a child's character, and so forth. They also provide accurate information on a pupil's date of birth, the father's name, occupation and abode.

School logbooks, governors' minute books and anniversary publications reveal detailed information about exam results, epidemics, the appointment of teaching staff, punishment records, the careers of former pupils, and school accounts. Often a school anniversary was mentioned in the local newspaper.

Franciscan Road Infants' School, Tooting, 1918
(courtesy of Mr. E. C. Cronin)

Apprentices

Apprentices were boys or girls bound by their parents to live with and work for an employer, in order to learn a craft or profession.

Register of apprentices from the Foundling Hospital, London, 1759 *(courtesy of the Governors of the Thomas Coram Foundation for Children and Corporation of London: London Metropolitan Archives, ref. A/FH/A12/1003/001 p12)*

Apprenticeship was a common practice from the Middle Ages right up to the mid-nineteenth century, and the terms of apprenticeship contracts were laid out in documents called 'indentures'.

'Poor Law' apprentices were pauper children who lived on the charity of the parish and were sent out to employers in order to learn a trade and cease to be a financial burden on the local community. Most of them were sent as servants to private homes or as labourers to large estates, though boys were also sent into the navy as cabin-boys, into the army as drummer-boys, or out to the Colonies.

Apprenticeship records are very useful to the family historian as they contain the names of the boy or girl, their father, family occupation, abode and status.

Where the records are

School records can be found in county record offices, in the offices of local education authorities, or at the school itself.

The Society of Genealogists holds many printed school registers and histories, as do local libraries.

'Apprenticeship Books' are the records of the Apprentice Duty Tax which was levied between 1710 and 1811, and are held at the Public Record Office at Kew.

Other useful apprenticeship records, some of which would originally have been kept in the parish chest, are to be found at the PRO, the Guildhall Library, the Society of Genealogists, and county record offices.

Records can also be found in the archives of some industries and charities.

Delinquent pauper children can often be traced in the records of the local quarter sessions, or corrective institutions such as training ships and farm schools.

Army

There has been a regular professional army in England since 1660. Few records survive from before this date, but they become progressively more comprehensive over the centuries.

To trace the service records of an ancestor in the British army, the family historian should first know the approximate dates and places of service and, if possible, his regiment.

In the case of soldiers who did not die in service but were discharged with a pension, the main records available are attestation (joining-up) and discharge papers, covering the period 1760–1913. These papers also contain details of place of birth, age on enlistment, physical appearance, usual trade, service, conduct and medical record.

Pension records reveal when and where pensions were paid, and when they stopped on the death of the recipient.

Age on enlistment, birthplace, and date and reason for discharge of those who died in service or left the regiment for other reasons, can usually be traced through muster rolls or regimental pay lists.

In the case of commissioned officers, the starting place for any search should be the *Army Lists*. These have been published almost every year since 1754, and you can trace an officer's career from the late 18th century onwards using commission papers, service returns and pension registers. You can frequently find out about his family here too.

The Public Record Office at Kew also has records of campaign and gallantry medals.

Discharge papers of Gunner John Hardy, 1876
(PRO ref. WO 97/1797)

The Battle of Glencoe (Natal Province, South Africa)
20th October 1899, between the British and Boer republicans
(PRO ref. COPY 1/158 f.385)

Where the records are

All are available at the Public Record Office at Kew, as well as many other types of documents which may give additional information about your ancestor.

Personal records of soldiers and officers who served or were commissioned up to 1920 are in the process of being transferred to the PRO over the next few years, but some 60% were lost in a bombing raid during World War II.

Later records are held by the Ministry of Defence.

Indexes of the deaths of English and Welsh servicemen in World Wars I and II, indexes to deaths in the Boer War (1899–1902) and indexes of births, marriages and deaths of Army personnel and their families from 1761, are to be found at the Family Records Centre.

Navy

English naval forces developed during the Middle Ages in order to protect the coasts against enemy attack and to carry troops abroad.

Henry VIII set up the Navy Board in 1546, and built a fleet of fighting ships, including the *Mary Rose*. Under Elizabeth I, the Navy developed into a major defence force and played a vital role in defeating the Spanish Armada in 1588. The title 'Royal' was given to British naval forces by Charles II.

There are relatively few records of the Navy before 1660. Even until quite recently, records are fragmented, so the more information you can obtain from other sources, the easier it will be to trace your ancestor.

Royal Navy

Information about commissioned officers can be found in the printed *Navy Lists* at the PRO at Kew, which run from 1782 up to the present day. These give a basic outline of an officer's career from lieutenant onwards. You may also be able to find his date and place of birth and death, marriage details, ships served on, summary of service and pension details from other records at Kew.

To trace a seaman in the Royal Navy before continuous engagement began in 1853, you usually need to know the name of at least one ship on which he served and the approximate date of service.

Royal Navy records at the PRO at Kew reveal such information as date of enlisting, age, place of birth, date of discharge or death, physical description, ships served on, summary of service and pension details.

Merchant Navy

Records about Masters and Mates in the Merchant Navy can reveal date and place of birth, year and capacity in which they first went to sea, details of ships and voyages, injuries, retirement or death.

For a merchant seaman, the records provide date and place of birth, age, date of first going to sea, rank, usual abode, and details of previous service.

Royal Marines

The Public Record Office at Kew also holds extensive records of the Royal Marines.

Service records of officers are available for the period 1793–1925, and give details of service and occasionally the name and profession of the officer's father.

If you are tracing an ancestor from the ranks, it is important to know which division he served in.

Description books, attestation forms and service records can provide place and date of birth, previous occupation, religion and physical description as well as details of service.

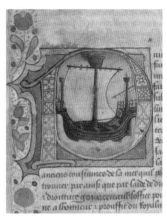

A 15th century ship depicted in an illuminated initial letter 'P' from the Black Book of the Admiralty, a book of rules from the Office of the Lord Admiral
(PRO ref. HCA 12/1)

Where the records are

The Public Record Office at Kew holds many records for officers and seamen of both the Royal and Merchant Navy, and the Royal Marines.

You may also be lucky and find your forebear as a crew member on board a Royal Naval or Merchant vessel enumerated in the census returns held at the Family Records Centre.

Indexes to Naval deaths in both World Wars are kept at the Family Records Centre.

Muster roll of HMS *Temeraire*, 1805
(PRO ref. ADM 36/15850)

Police

The modern police force has developed since the Metropolitan Police was set up in 1829, and the County Police Act was passed in 1839. The Irish Constabulary was created in 1836, and re-named the Royal Irish Constabulary in 1867. It was disbanded in 1922.

City of London Police officers forming part of the
Lord Mayor's Show, 1885 *(PRO ref. COPY 1/69 f.134)*

The survival of records for policemen is very patchy, although some recruitment, retirement and pension registers do exist for the Metropolitan Police, and indexed Royal Irish Constabulary records contain very detailed information.

Arrest of the men accused
of the Hanwell murder, 1899
(PRO ref. COPY 1/440A)

Before then, manors and parishes appointed unpaid parish constables to maintain the peace, with varying degrees of efficiency. In 1856, all cities, boroughs and counties were obliged to set up police forces of their own, although many had already done so in the 1830s and 1840s. Since then, smaller local borough police forces have been gradually absorbed into countywide forces.

Metropolitan Police service record, 1894–1920 *(PRO ref. MEPO 4/389)*

Where the records are

Metropolitan Police and Royal Irish Constabulary records are held at the Public Record Office at Kew.

The Metropolitan Police Historical Museum (currently in storage) can also answer telephone or written enquiries from family historians.

Police records of other forces are not public records, but may be deposited in county record offices, or are retained by the local force itself.

Names of parish constables appear in parish records, such as vestry minutes, and county quarter session records.

Crime and punishment

It has always been a primary duty of the state to protect the citizen from wrongdoers and to provide justice for those who require it. This has meant that a great many records relating to the legal system have been created over the centuries.

If you are interested in tracing the criminal career of an ancestor, it is important to know, or be able to hazard a guess about, where and when he or she was tried, and what the offence was. With this knowledge, you can often find a wealth of fascinating and sometimes detailed information about the life and treatment of offenders.

For the nineteenth and early part of the twentieth century there are annual registers of people indicted to appear at the assizes or quarter sessions, and lists of prisoners, by gaol. It is much easier to work back to the court records from these documents rather than vice-versa.

You should bear in mind that records created by some courts may be difficult to use. They often show little more than the progress of a case through the courts, rather than a verbatim account of the trial. Before 1733, legal records were written in often heavily abbreviated Latin, and can be difficult to read.

Wormwood Scrubs Prison whipping post. Photographed by William Grove in 1895.
(PRO ref. COPY 1/420i)

Police discharge papers of a 14 year old girl convicted of larceny in 1893 *(PRO ref. PCOM 2/291/411)*

Where the records are

They are split between the Public Record Office at Kew and local record offices, and it is not always clear what is held where.

The PRO holds records of:

- Central courts, for both criminal and civil matters such as:
  Assizes
  High courts
  Chancery
  Exchequer
  King's Bench
  Court of Common Pleas
- Central Criminal Court for London (known as the Old Bailey before 1834)
- Annual criminal registers 1791–1892. Of particular interest are the registers of habitual criminals
- Registers or calendars of prisoners covering the whole country, including prison hulks
- Bankrupts and debtors
- Transportation registers of convicts

Local record offices usually hold records of:

- Petty sessions (magistrates or police courts)
  Quarter sessions (local criminal and civil courts) to 1972
  Crown courts (criminal) from 1972
- County courts (local civil courts)
- County constabulary
- Gaol calendars and registers of local prisoners
- Coroners' proceedings

Poor Law

The old Poor Law came into effect in 1601, under Elizabeth I. Administered by Overseers of the Poor, it formally established the raising of money from households to shelter, feed and care for the poor of a particular parish. In 1834 the Poor Law Act grouped parishes into Poor Law Unions, each with its own workhouse.

Those who received help were known as 'paupers' and help was originally provided in people's own houses as 'out relief.'

After 1834, however, to obtain help people had to go into the workhouse, where they were oppressed by the harsh conditions and petty regulations imposed on them. The sexes were segregated and children were separated from their parents. Dickens' novel *Oliver Twist* provides us with a vivid description of workhouse life.

If you are not sure whether your ancestor was a pauper, you may find he or she is identified as such in certificates or census records.

The Poor Law itself and its application generated a great deal of detailed record-keeping.

Bastardy sworn examination, St. Leonard, Shoreditch, 1766 *(courtesy of Corporation of London: London Metropolitan Archives, ref. P91/LEN/1201p.118)*

Order of removal from parish, St. Leonard, Shoreditch, 1842 *(courtesy of Corporation of London: London Metropolitan Archives, ref. P91/LEN/1263p.185)*

Cartoon attacking the Poor Law, 1834 *(PRO ref. EXT 6/1)*

You can often find much personal information on your ancestor, such as place and date of birth, parentage, pensions received, medical details, physical description, children's work, and many other facets of a usually bleak existence.

Where the records are

Most Poor Law records are at county record offices, where you should start your search.

The Public Record Office at Kew has almost no Poor Law records before 1834. After that date, however, you can find much information about paupers seeking assistance, in the Poor Law Union records. There is also limited information about workhouse officers.

Census records may be useful in tracing and identifying inmates and staff of workhouses, schools or asylums. These are available at the Family Records Centre.

Newspapers

Newspapers, both national and local, can provide valuable information to the family historian.

Newspapers give a contemporary account of past events and insights into social conditions. Advertisements, reports of fatalities or obituaries may reveal previously unknown information about ancestors. Two of the earliest newspapers were:

The London Gazette, which was first published in 1665, shortly after the restoration of the monarchy. The Gazette was used to publicise Government activities and official information.

It listed bankruptcies, clerical preferments, service promotions, decorations, citations, statutes, and Crown and Government appointments.

The Gentleman's Magazine, which first came out in 1731 and remained in print until the early twentieth century. It published news of births, marriages and deaths of members of the gentry, as well as articles of general interest and entertainment value.

Sir John Coulson, KCMG, Secretary-General of the European Free Trade Association (Efta) 1965-72, died on November 15 aged 88. He was born on September 13, 1909.

AS A clerk in the Foreign Office, John Coulson was responsible for sending off th-

Obituary from *The Times*

Where the records are

The London Gazette and *The Gentleman's Magazine* can both be seen at the Public Record Office at Kew, and at the Guildhall Library.

Microfilm copies of *The Times* are also available at the Public Record Office, and in many local libraries.

The main newspaper and magazine repository for England and Wales is the British Library Newspaper Library at Colindale.

Most local libraries have copies of newspapers from their immediate area.

Newspaper boy, 1900 (*PRO ref. COPY 1/447*)

The Gentleman's Magazine, 1731

Electoral registers

Electoral registers or 'rolls' are lists of people eligible to vote in an election.

Electoral registers were established under the Reform Act of 1832, which gave the vote to men who owned or occupied land or property over a certain value. Subsequent Acts in 1867, 1884 and 1918, which modified the eligibility criteria, gradually allowed more men to vote. In 1918 all women over 30 and men over 21 were given the franchise.

The Representation of the People Act, 1928 gave the vote to all women over 21. In 1969, the voting age was lowered to 18.

Electoral registers are important tools for the genealogist. They can establish residency, and dates of birth can be calculated according to when names first appear.

Poll books

Before 1872, 'poll books' recorded by name the votes of individuals, but they were not published in all constituencies. They include the individual's address if it is different to the qualifying property.

Poll Book, Oxfordshire, 1754

Members of the Suffragette movement, 1906.
Right: Christabel Pankhurst, daughter of Emmeline.
Left: believed to be Annie Kenney (*PRO ref. COPY 1/494*)

Where the records are

The British Library holds copies of most electoral registers.

County record offices and local history archives also tend to hold copies for their own areas, and a run of electoral registers for some years in the 1870s is available in the PRO library at Kew.

Current registers can be seen at local town halls (sometimes with earlier copies), libraries and post offices. A set for England and Wales, dating from about a year ago, can be seen at the Family Records Centre, on the ground floor.

Some poll books, which record how people voted, are held at county record offices and the Society of Genealogists, but the major collections are with the Guildhall Library and the Institute of Historical Research, both in London.

Maps

Maps can be very helpful in building up a picture of your ancestors, if you know the town or county where they lived. They may confirm land ownership, and can bring to life information about property changing hands, perhaps as an inheritance.

Four main categories of maps are used in genealogical research:

Ordnance Survey maps
In 1791, the government began the first survey of Great Britain, using the expertise of the branch of the British army known as the Ordnance, or Artillery. The maps were highly accurate, and updated versions are still published.

Tithe maps
Tithe maps were drawn up between 1836 and about 1850. They were the result of the Tithe Commission, set up to convert payment of the tithe to the parish priest (a tenth of the annual produce of a person's land) into money. Special Tithe Commissioners travelled through the country holding parish meetings to settle the terms of commutation, based on land occupancy and corn prices. The maps show each affected property, and Tithe Apportionments the landowners' liabilities.

Enclosure Award maps
Many Enclosure Award maps were compiled long before Tithe maps. They defined the new ownership of what had been common land, and were used to calculate compensation for those affected by the 'enclosing' of land by private landowners.

Valuation Office maps
These were produced between 1910 and 1915 for taxation purposes. They were adapted from Ordnance Survey maps, with plot numbers of each property linked to field books.

15th century map of Chertsey Abbey and its estates, probably produced in an effort to settle a dispute over pasturing rights
(PRO ref. E 164/25f222)

Field book used to record Valuation Office data 1910–1915
(PRO ref. IR 58/4567)

Where the records are

Some Ordnance Survey maps are available at the PRO at Kew and at the Family Records Centre, but for a comprehensive set you will need to go to a large deposit library, such as the British Library.

Tithe maps are held at the PRO at Kew and there are also copies in county record offices.

Enclosure Award maps are held at the PRO, the House of Lords Record Office and local record offices.

Valuation Office record maps and field books are held at the PRO at Kew.

Taxation

Taxes are moneys collected by the Crown or local authorities to finance their activities.

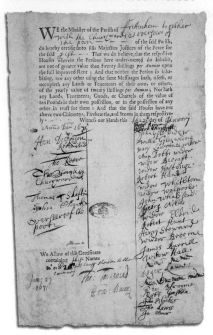

Hearth Tax certificate of persons unable to pay their assessment, 1671

Most surviving records relate to property, so it helps to know where your ancestor lived. Once you know this, tax returns can be a good source of information about conditions of life, social status, residential continuity, surname distribution and mobility. The vast majority of records which are available for consultation are for the nineteenth century or earlier.

Lay Subsidy
Starting in 1290, these records list names of assessed tax payers. After 1332 however, no names are recorded until the tax was revamped by Henry VIII in 1523, and levied on an individual's wealth in goods, annual income from land, or wages.

This was superseded by the Hearth Tax.

Hearth Tax
From 1662 to 1689, occupiers of houses were taxed 2/- (two shillings) on each of their hearths (fireplaces). The poor were exempt, but were frequently listed.

Window Tax
Between 1696 and 1851, a tax was levied on the number of windows in a house.
A few records have survived.

Land Tax
A tax on land was collected annually between 1692 and 1949. Payment was calculated according to the value of estates or lands owned by individuals.

The lists of assessed payers will reveal the names of occupiers, landlords, the amount levied, and occasionally give a brief description of the property.

Poll Tax
There are sporadic lists of men and women liable for this tax, detailing how much they owe, for 1377, 1379, 1381 and between 1640 and 1698. The records give the parish where those who were liable lived.

Rates
Rates were a local tax based on the value of a property.

Surviving records, called rate books, dating from the 18th century onwards, usually list the householder, landlord, amounts levied and when paid, and a description of the premises.

Valuation Office Records
In 1909, the Valuation Office was set up to assess the value of all land and buildings in the United Kingdom with a view to introducing a new tax.

Field books give details of owners, occupiers and tenancies, property descriptions and valuations.

Valuation books contain similar details excluding property descriptions.

Domesday Book 1086, the great survey of land holdings and tax liability
(PRO ref. E 31/2)

Where the records are

Most of these assessments and tax returns are at the Public Record Office at Kew. Others are held at local record offices.

The few Window Tax returns that have survived are mostly available at local record offices, as are all existing Land Tax assessments, except Land Tax for the year 1798, which is kept at the PRO at Kew.

Rate books are at local record offices.

Valuation Office field books and record maps are at the PRO at Kew, while valuation books are almost all at county record offices.

Further reading

Bevan, A., *Tracing Your Ancestors in the Public Record Office* (PRO, 5th edition, 1999)

Breed, G.R., *My Ancestors were Baptists* (Society of Genealogists, 3rd edition, 1995)

Cale, M., *Law and Society: An Introduction to Sources for Criminal and Legal History from 1800* (PRO Readers' Guide No 14, 1996)

Camp, A., *Wills and Their Whereabouts* (London, 1974)

Chapman, C.R., *The Growth of British Education and its Records* (Lochin Publishing, 2nd edition, 1992)

Chapman, C.R., *Using Newspapers and Periodicals* (FFHS, 1993)

Clifford, D.J.H., *My Ancestors were Congregationalists* (Society of Genealogists, 2nd edition, 1997)

Collins, A., *Basic Facts About Using the Family Records Centre* (FFHS, 1997)

Colwell, S., *Teach Yourself Tracing Your Family History* (Hodder & Stoughton, 1997)

Cox, J. & Colwell, S., *Never Been Here Before? A Genealogists' Guide to the Family Records Centre* (PRO Readers' Guide No 17, 1997)

Federation of Family History Societies, *British Isles Genealogical Register* (FFHS, 1997)

Foot, W., *Maps for Family History* (PRO Readers' Guide No 9, 1994)

Fowler, S. & Spencer, W., *Army Records for Family Historians* (PRO Readers' Guide No 2, 2nd edition,1998)

Fowler, S., Spencer, W. & Tamblin, S., *Army Service Records of the First World War* (PRO Readers' Guide No 19, 1997)

Gandy, M., *Catholic Missions and Registers, 1700–1880* (Whetstone, 6 vols., 1993)

Gibson, J.S.W., *The Hearth Tax, Other Later Stuart Tax Lists, and the Association Oath Rolls* (FFHS, 2nd edition, 1996)

Gibson, J.S.W., *Bishops' Transcripts and Marriage Licences* (FFHS, 4th edition, 1997)

Gibson, J.S.W., *Local Newspapers, 1750–1920: England & Wales, Channel Islands, Isle of Man: A Select Location List* (FFHS, 1989)

Gibson, J.S.W., *Quarter Sessions Records for Family Historians* (FFHS, 4th edition, 1995)

Gibson, J.S.W., *Probate Jurisdictions: Where to Look for Wills* (FFHS, 4th edition, 1997)

Gibson, J.S.W. & Dell, A., *Tudor and Stuart Muster Rolls* (FFHS, 1991)

Gibson, J.S.W. & Hampson, E., *Marriage and Census Indexes for Family Historians* (FFHS, 7th edition, 1998)

Gibson, J.S.W. & Hampson, E., *Census Returns 1841–1891 in Microform: A Directory to Local Holdings in Great Britain, Channel Islands and the Isle of Man* (FFHS, 6th edition, 1997)

Gibson, J.S.W. & Medlycott, M., *Local Census Listings 1522–1930* (FFHS, 3rd edition, 1997)

Gibson, J.S.W. & Medlycott, M., *Militia Lists and Musters, 1757–1876* (FFHS, 3rd edition, 1994)

Gibson, J.S.W., Medlycott, M. & Mills, D., *Land and Window Tax Assessments* (FFHS, 2nd edition, 1998)

Gibson, J.S.W. & Peskett, P., *Record Offices: How to Find Them* (FFHS, 8th edition, 1998)

Gibson, J.S.W. & Rogers, C., *Poor Law Union Records* (FFHS, 4 vols, 1993)

Gibson, J.S.W. & Rogers, C., *Electoral Registers since 1832 and Burgess Rolls: A Directory to Holdings in Great Britain* (FFHS, 2nd edition, 1990)

Gibson, J.S.W. & Rogers, C., *Poll Books c.1696–1872: A Directory to Holdings in Great Britain* (FFHS, 3rd edition, 1994)

Gibson, J.S.W. & Rogers, C., *Coroners' Records in England and Wales* (FFHS, 2nd edition, 1997)

Hawkings, D.T., *Criminal Ancestors: A Guide to Historical Criminal Records in England and Wales* (Alan Sutton, 1992)

Herber, M.D., *Ancestral Trails* (Alan Sutton, 1997)

Herlihy, J., *The Royal Irish Constabulary, A Short History and Genealogical Guide* (Four Courts Press, 1997)

Hey, D., *The Oxford Companion to Local and Family History* (OUP, 1996)

Higgs, E., *A Clearer Sense of the Census* (HMSO, 1996)

Humphrey-Smith, C. (ed.), *Phillimore Atlas & Index of Parish Registers* (Phillimore, 2nd edition, 1995)

Johnson, K.A. & Sainty, M.R., *Genealogical Research Directory* (North Sydney, annual, 1981–)

Leary, W., *My Ancestors were Methodists* (Society of Genealogists, 3rd edition, 1999)

Lumas, S., *Making Use of the Census* (PRO Readers' Guide No 1, 3rd edition, 1997)

McKinley, R.A., *A History of British Surnames* (Addison-Wesley Longman, 1990)

McLaughlin, E., *Parish Registers* (McLaughlin, 3rd edition, 1994)

Milligan, E.H. & Thomas, M.J., *My Ancestors were Quakers* (Society of Genealogists, 2nd edition, 1999)

Mordy, I., *My Ancestors were Jewish* (Society of Genealogists, 2nd edition, 1995

Nissel, M., *People Count: A History of the General Register Office* (HMSO, 1987)

Pelling, G., *Beginning Your Family History* (Countryside Books and FFHS, 7th edition, 1998)

Reaney, P.H. & Wilson, R.M., *Dictionary of English Surnames* (RKP, 3rd edition, 1991)

Rodger, N.A.M., *Naval Records for Genealogists* (PRO Handbook No 22, 1998)

Ruston, A., *My Ancestors were English Presbyterians/ Unitarians* (Society of Genealogists, 1993)

Saul, P., *The Family Historian's Enquire Within* (FFHS, 5th edition, 1995)

Scott, M., *Prerogative Court of Canterbury Wills and Other Probate Records* (PRO Readers' Guide No 15, 1997)

Shorney, D., *Protestant Nonconformity and Roman Catholicism* (PRO Readers' Guide No 13, 1996)

Smith, K., Watts, C.T. & Watts, M.J., *Records of Merchant Shipping and Seamen* (PRO Readers' Guide No 20, 1998)

Society of Genealogists, *School, University and College Registers and Histories in the Library of the Society of Genealogists* (Society of Genealogists, 2nd edition, 1996)

Spencer, W., *Records of the Militia and Volunteer Forces 1757–1945* (PRO Readers' Guide No 3, 1997)

Tate, W.E., *The Parish Chest* (Phillimore, 3rd edition, 1983)

Thomas, G., *Records of the Royal Marines* (PRO Readers' Guide No 10, 1994)

Todd, A., *Basic Sources for Family History* (Allen & Todd, 3rd edition, 1995)

Willings, *Press Guide* (annual)

Wood, T., *Introduction to Civil Registration* (FFHS, 1994)

Names and addresses

Borthwick Institute of Historical Research
St. Anthony's Hall,
Peasholme Green,
York YO1 2PW
(Tel: 01904 642315 www.york.ac.uk/inst/bihr)

British Isles Family History Service Centre
185 Penns Lane,
Sutton Coldfield,
Birmingham B76 1JU
(Tel: 0121 384 2028 http://lds.org/)

British Library
96 Euston Road,
London NW1 2DB
(Tel: 0171 412 7000 www.bl.uk)

British Library Newspaper Library
Colindale Avenue,
London NW9 5HE
(Tel: 0171 412 7353)

Church of Jesus Christ of Latter-day Saints
Family History Centre,
64/68 Exhibition Road,
London SW7 2PA
(Tel: 0171 589 8561 www.familysearch.com)

Corporation of London Record Office
Guildhall,
London EC2P 2EJ
(Tel: 0171 606 3030 www.cityoflondon.gov.uk)

Federation of Family History Societies
The Benson Room,
Birmingham and Midland Institute,
Margaret Street,
Birmingham B3 3BS
(Tel: 07041 49032 www.ffhs.org.uk/)

General Register Office for Scotland
New Register House,
Edinburgh EH1 3YT
(Tel: 0131 334 0380 www.open.gov.uk/gros/)

Guild of One-Name Studies
c/o Box G,
14 Charterhouse Buildings,
Goswell Road,
London EC1M 7BA

Guildhall Library
Aldermanbury,
London EC2P 2EJ
(Tel: 0171 606 3030 www.cityoflondon.gov.uk)

House of Lords Record Office
Westminster,
London SW1A 0PW
(Tel: 0171 219 3074 www.parliament.uk)

Institute of Historical Research
University of London,
Senate House,
Malet Street,
London WC1E 7HU
(Tel: 0171 636 0272 www.ihrinfo.ac.uk)

London Metropolitan Archives
40 Northampton Road,
London EC1R 0HB
(Tel: 0171 332 3820)

Metropolitan Police Historical Museum
c/o Room 1317,
New Scotland Yard,
London SW1H 0BG
(Tel: 0181 305 2824)

Ministry of Defence
Bourne Avenue,
Hayes,
Middlesex UB3 1RF
(Tel: 0181 573 3831)

The National Archives of Ireland
Bishop Street,
Dublin 8
(Tel: 00 3531 4783711 www.nationalarchives.ie/)

Office for National Statistics
General Register Office,
Smedley Hydro,
Trafalgar Road,
Southport,
Merseyside PR8 2HH
(Tel: 0151 471 4800)

*Postal applications for birth, marriage and death
certificates after 1837*

Probate Search Room
First Avenue House,
42-9 High Holborn,
London WC1V 6HA
(Tel: 0171 936 7000)

Public Record Office
Kew, Richmond,
Surrey TW9 4DU
(Tel: 0181 876 3444 www.pro.gov.uk/)

Public Record Office of Northern Ireland
66 Balmoral Avenue,
Belfast BT9 6NY
(Tel: 01232 661621 proni.nics.gov.uk/)

Society of Genealogists
14 Charterhouse Buildings,
Goswell Road,
London EC1M 7BA
(Tel: 0171 251 8799 www.sog.org.uk)